CONTENTS

snapping-turtle guide

COPYRIGHT © 2004

ticktock ENTERTAINMENT LTD UK

website @ **www.ticktock.co.uk**

THE ERECHTHEION

These magnificent caryatid statues, overlooking Athens, are part of the Erechtheion temple on the Acropolis. Built over 2,400 years ago, they are an impressive reminder of the ancient Greeks and their culture.

GREEK LIFE

BY

JOHN GUY

Who were the Ancient Greeks?

A ncient Greece is regarded by many as the cradle of civilization in Europe but unlike Rome and other civilizations that followed, it did not consist of one centrally controlled empire. Early Greek civilizations were greatly influenced by nearby Egypt and Sumeria. The first of these was the Minoan, centred on the island of Crete, which flourished between *c.*2000-1400 BC. On the Greek mainland, the dominant civilization was the Mycenaean, *c.*1600-1100 BC. After that, Greece entered a 'Dark Age', of which very little is known, until the emergence in the 8th century BC of a number of independent city-states. Each one forged links with, and was influenced by the others. They in turn rose to power, usually by invasion rather than by agreement. As each did so, new sites were chosen for their cities, which has resulted in many sites lying undisturbed over the centuries, albeit in ruins as locals frequently raided them for building materials. The result of this pattern of development has enabled historians and archaeologists to peel back these various layers of civilization and view them in isolation.

PULLING TOGETHER

Although the Greek city-states acted independently, one of the rare times they worked together was in the Trojan Wars *c.*1184 BC. The Mycenaean king, Agamemnon, united the Greeks against Troy, defeating them with the use of a huge wooden horse.

GREEK TOWNS

The centre of every Greek town followed very much the same plan. Built on hills for defence, the civic and religious buildings were close together as they were central to Greek society.

THE TEMPLE

The main temple usually occupied the highest point of the acropolis and was intended to impress both the people and the gods.

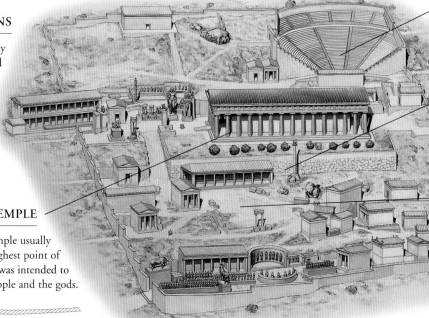

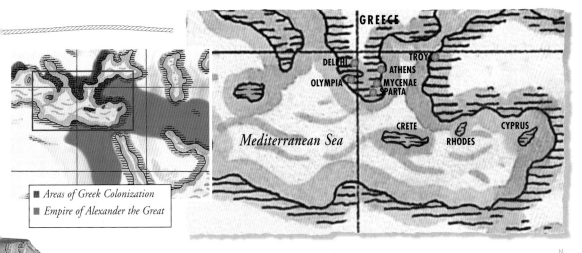

GREECE

DELPHI
TROY
ATHENS
OLYMPIA
MYCENAE
SPARTA

CRETE
RHODES
CYPRUS

Mediterranean Sea

■ *Areas of Greek Colonization*
■ *Empire of Alexander the Great*

SPIRITUAL CENTRE

The Omphalos Stone (shown here) was thought to mark the centre of the universe. According to myth, Zeus wanted to measure the world so he set two eagles free from opposite ends of the Earth. They met over Delphi so Zeus decreed that this was the world's centre, and the site assumed profound religious importance.

THE FIRST EUROPEANS

The earliest known civilization in Europe flourished on Crete in the eastern Mediterranean. It was named Minoan, after the legendary King Minos who was said to rule the Aegean sea. Excavations of the palace of Knossos in northern Crete have revealed that its inhabitants enjoyed a sophisticated lifestyle. It was highly decorated and had an advanced drainage and water-supply system.

THE AMPHITHEATRE

Every major town had an open-air theatre, called an amphitheatre.

THE ACROPOLIS

At the highest point of the town was a citadel or walled enclosure. This housed the most important town buildings; the temples and government buildings.

THE AGORA

In the centre was the *agora*, a large open space where people met and conducted business.

THE COLOSSUS OF RHODES

Once part of Macedonia, in *c.*408 BC the islanders of Rhodes formed themselves into an independent state. The island was unsuccessfully besieged by Demetrios in 305-304 BC, following the removal of a Macedonian garrison by the Rhodians. To mark their victory they built the Colossus, a gigantic statue of the sun god, Helios. It stood 31 metres high and straddled the harbour entrance. One of the 'Seven Wonders of the World', it was destroyed by an earthquake in *c.*227 BC.

FINE CRAFTSMANSHIP

As food was easily available at the town's market, not everyone needed to grow their own. Workers could develop other skills to trade and the Greek potters became fine craftsmen.

Using local clay, they produced beautifully decorated items including plates, dishes, wine goblets, bottles and vases for both the home market and for export. Many of these items have survived intact, and the intricate designs tell us much about the Greek lifestyle.

ELEGANT CLOTHES

This carved relief from a temple shows the typical clothes worn by the wealthier Greeks. Whereas the poor had to rely on home-spun linen or woollen clothes, the rich could afford to buy exotic imported materials, such as fine cotton and silk from India and the East. The rich employed the services of tailors or bought ready-made clothes from merchants. Both sexes wore a *chitan* made from two large pieces of rectangular material fastened at the sides and neck, but worn loose, like a tunic. Women wore their clothes to ankle length; men to the knee.

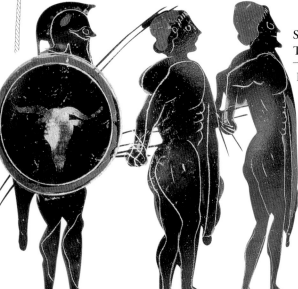

SLAVE TRADE

Like most ancient civilizations, Greece relied heavily on slave labour. Slavery served two main purposes: it showed the superiority of the victorious Greeks over the peoples of conquered lands, and big money was made by selling slaves to wealthy Greeks as servants and cheap labour.

Life for the Rich

The rich mostly lived in large town houses, conveniently close to all the town's facilities. The very rich might also have had a house in the country. Despite the often grand designs of Greek civic buildings and temples, homes were not particularly ornate – the rich just had larger houses with more rooms than those of the poor. Most wealthy men were engaged in government or commerce, so it was essential to live in towns in order to conduct their business. For the wives of wealthy men, the house was virtually a prison. Slaves carried out the mundane domestic duties that usually brought women into contact with others, so few ventured out without their husbands.

SIMPLE TASTES

Houses, even for the rich, were basic, made from dried mud bricks (painted white to deflect the heat of the sun) or stone. They had tiled roofs, stone floors and a small open courtyard, perhaps containing a private well. Windows were few, to keep the interior cool and shady. The rooms were simply but comfortably furnished, as this vase illustration shows. Their beds had mattresses, pillows and bedding, and other furniture included tables and footstools.

DEATH MASK

This beautiful mask of beaten gold was believed to be the funerary mask of Agamemnon, the legendary king of Mycenae who died in the 12th century BC. In fact, it is probably much older than that, possibly 500 years older. Such masks were commonly used in royal burials and show the wealth of the Mycenaean civilization at the time.

RAISE YOUR GLASS

The technique of glass-blowing was not perfected until Roman times. Prior to that, glass was an expensive commodity and difficult to work. Most drinking vessels were made of clay, therefore, but the rich would buy goblets made of glass to show their wealth and impress their friends.

Life for the Poor

Although most of the remains from ancient Greece are grand, in terms of both scale and design, this gives a rather misguided view of their society. A fortunate few were wealthy and enjoyed a luxurious lifestyle, but most of the population were poor, carving their meagre living from the land as best they could. The barren Greek soils and dry climate often gave poor harvests, and peasants were sometimes forced to leave the poorer regions and help populate the new colonies in the empire rather than face starvation. However hard-working, people of all classes took their leisure time seriously. Many religious festivals coincided with the bringing in of the harvest, when everyone in the village joined in and celebrated the season's crop.

EARTHENWARE

Pottery for the poorer classes was much simpler, less decorative and more functional than for the rich. Life was a struggle for existence and there was little time or money to expend on unnecessary luxuries. Plates, pots and drinking vessels were usually made from unglazed clay, moulded by hand and left to dry in the sun.

BEASTS OF BURDEN

The most common beast of burden was the donkey or mule. They are very sure-footed animals which was particularly important in the mountainous and rocky terrain of Greece. Peasant farmers often used their donkeys to travel considerable distances from villages to reach their fields. Donkeys were also used as pack animals, as they still are today in the poorer regions of Greece, to take produce to market in the towns. For the very poor who could not afford an ox, donkeys were even used to pull the plough.

ALL PULL TOGETHER

The Greeks did not operate a centrally organized system of agriculture. Each farmer grew his own food and had his own oxen to pull the plough. Poorer communities would sometimes share a team of oxen, with each family taking its turn. In order to help feed the growing population, it was necessary for the Greeks to expand their empire. They set up colonies around the Mediterranean to enable Greek merchants to import any shortfall in food supply. They would trade luxury goods in exchange for grain.

HUMBLE HOMES

For the poor, houses were simple, with few concessions to luxury. They were built from dried mud bricks, plastered with wet mud and painted white to deflect the summer heat. Window openings were few and unglazed and roofs were either thatched or tiled. The construction and style was not hugely different from houses and churches still seen in Greece today. They would have had only one main room where the entire family lived and ate. Communal bedrooms occupied a loft-like upper floor and furnishings were few, usually comprising just a table, chairs and beds.

SUBSISTENCE FARMING

The majority of the population lived in remote villages, scattered throughout the land and often separated from one another by the mountains. Peasants eked out a subsistence form of farming, each growing just enough to feed their own family. Fortunately, most communities were located close to the sea so the poor could supplement their diet with fresh seafood. Any surplus of food was taken to market to trade for other commodities, such as shoes and wine. Most families, including the poorer townsfolk, would also keep a few goats for milk and cheese and chickens for eggs.

LEISURE TIME

One of the most popular pastimes in ancient Greece was attending plays, pageants or festivals at the town's amphitheatre. Performances were free or inexpensive, subsidised by rich benefactors or politicians who wished to win favour with the populace, and so even the poor could enjoy the festivities. Women were not encouraged to attend, though they were probably not actually banned from doing so, but they were certainly excluded from taking part in the performances. To become an actor was one of the few means of escape from the drudgery of poverty for boys.

SEAFOOD

The Mediterranean is abundant with seafood, particularly
octopus and squid, which still forms an important part of Greek cuisine today.
The usual method of cooking was to cut the tentacles into small slices and to boil or fry
them in olive oil. Common fish still caught in Greek waters are tuna, mullet and mackerel.

ARBRES FRUITIERS.

Récolte des olives.

VÉRITABLE EXTRAIT DE VIANDE LIEBIG.

OLIVE GROVES

The goddess Athena supposedly introduced the olive tree into Greece.
Olives were either eaten or pressed to make oil, used in cooking,
rubbed into the skin, or burnt for lighting. Olive trees grow
profusely in Greece and still provide a valuable source of
income for farmers today.

VINTAGE WINE

The most common drink for Greeks of all
classes was wine. Sometimes this was drunk
undiluted, but usually water was added
because of the vast quantities consumed.
The wine was quite thick and did not
keep well; it was usually
strained before drinking.
The Greeks knew the
importance of a clean
water supply, and
sometimes wine was
also used as a means
of purifying water.

HOME COOKING

This terracotta figure from Crete, made
in the 6th century BC, shows a woman
stirring food in a saucepan with a
ladle. She may be making stew, or
perhaps porridge. Vegetables were
often made into a stew and eaten with
bread, but the Greeks also enjoyed
salads dressed with garlic and olive oil.
Cooking was often done outdoors, to
avoid smells and the risk of fire. Inside, meals
were cooked on stone hearths using charcoal to
grill the food. Clay ovens were used for baking.

Food & Drink

As in most societies, ancient and modern, the wealthy Greeks ate very well, enjoying a wide variety of foods, while the poor had to make do with a more limited diet. However, all Greeks knew the importance of good food to their health, and they had a balanced diet consisting of protein, roughage, vegetables and dairy produce. Most people in rural areas grew their own food and tended their own animals. Even in towns many households kept a goat for fresh milk and cheese, and perhaps a few chickens for eggs. Meat was not widely eaten by the poor, except perhaps at religious festivals, but the rich enjoyed a variety of meats, including boar, deer and rabbit. Fortunately the waters of the Mediterranean provided a bountiful supply of seafood for everyone. Wine and water were the most common drinks. Fruit juices, such as fig juice, or honey were used to sweeten food. Herbs and spices from the East were used to garnish vegetables and salads, or to disguise the often rancid taste of rotten food.

SOURCE OF PROTEIN

As many settlements were sited near the coast, the sea provided a plentiful supply of alternative protein to meat, which the poor could not afford.

DAILY BREAD

The staple diet for many Greeks was bread made with wheat or barley flour. Greek bread was quite coarse and stodgy and was baked in flat, round loaves. A great favourite at breakfast-time was to soak bread in olive oil or wine, and eat it with figs or other fruit. The decorative loaf shown here was probably made for a banquet.

MUSIC AND DANCE

Music and dancing were popular with Greeks from all classes, not only as a pastime but also at religious festivals. Musicians often accompanied plays at the theatre or performed at private banquets. Common musical instruments of the time included flutes, pan-pipes, harps and lyres.

THEATRE-GOING

Most Greek cities had an amphitheatre at their centre. This was an open-air theatre where plays or enactments of stories of the gods and legendary heroes were popular. The plays were usually comedies or tragedies, and all the actors wore a mask to depict their character. Simple scene changes also added an air of mystery to the entertainment. All actors were men, with boys playing the women's roles.

LEGENDARY HEROES

One of the principal pastimes in the home was storytelling. Children would gather round to hear their parents recount legendary tales of past Greek heroes, or of the exploits of the gods. One such story is of Theseus slaying the Minotaur, a hybrid monster, half-bull, half-man, kept by the legendary King Minos in a labyrinth at Knossos, Crete.

DISCUS THROWING

Statues depicting discus throwing seem to have been popular, and perhaps these athletes represent the spirit of the Olympic Games more than any other. Like other events, discus throwing has its origins in warfare, as a means of training soldiers to hurl objects with accuracy at an enemy. The discus was generally larger and heavier those used today, and was made of stone or bronze.

THE OLYMPIC GAMES

The most important sporting event in ancient Greece was the Olympic Games, first established in 776 BC. Held on a rota basis every four years, the games were staged in Olympia and were conceived as a means of honouring the gods. Inevitably they became an outward show of the rivalry between the various city-states. Athletes travelled from far and wide to compete. Winning athletes brought honour to their home state and enjoyed celebrity status. In 1896 the ideal of the Olympic Games was revived and the first modern games were held in this stadium in Athens.

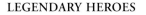

Pastimes

We know a great deal about how the ancient Greeks spent their leisure time because of the abundance of surviving art and artefacts depicting scenes of everyday life. Greek culture was based on a slave society, with captured slaves from newly-conquered lands performing many of the menial tasks. This left many Greeks, particularly the rich, with plenty of time on their hands. Leisure was seen as an essential part of everyday life, especially sporting activities which were regarded as necessary for good health. Sports also provided an important method of training for warfare and as a means of honouring the gods. Music, dancing and theatre-going were other popular pastimes, as were board games, gambling and horse and chariot racing.

THE JAVELIN THROWER

This stone relief depicts a Greek javelin thrower. Javelins were long, light spears specially balanced for throwing, and were originally made as a form of weapon training. It became one of the most popular events at sporting games.

Fashion

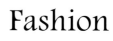

Greeks of all classes were very conscious of their appearance and spent a great deal of their time and money on their hairstyles, clothes and jewellery. The rivalry between the various city-states even extended to fashion – the people of one state believing themselves more sophisticated than the others. Clothes were often white or brightly coloured. For the poorer classes, finely-spun woollen textiles were common, while the rich displayed their wealth by importing exotic fabrics from the East, such as silk and cotton. The Greeks seemed quite unselfconscious about their bodies. Athletes, both male and female, usually performed naked and women's clothing was often made of light, transparent materials which, although cool to wear, could also be quite revealing.

ELABORATE HAIRSTYLES

Women used decorative pins and slides to hold their hair in place, while for men it was fashionable to curl their hair, as shown here.

NOVELTY VALUE

This beautiful perfume pot, made of decorated clay with a wax stopper, was probably made in either Corinth or Rhodes. Both regions were renowned for producing unusual novelty ware, such as this, for export. Greeks were quite fastidious about their personal hygiene and both men and women wore perfume.

PROPER DRESS

We know a great deal about the clothes worn by ordinary men and women from the beautiful decorations on Greek pottery, such as on this vase. Clothes for both sexes were quite similar, consisting of simple tunics, fastened at the shoulder by a brooch. Women tended to wear their clothes longer as it was considered improper to wear them short.

AN AGE OF ELEGANCE

Jewellery was popular amongst all classes and was often an indication of a person's wealth. Poorer people wore jewellery made of cheaper materials, such as bronze or ceramics. The rich preferred to use jewellery made of gold or silver. Although precious and semi-precious stones were used, Greek jewellers preferred to use delicately crafted gold and silver pendants and chains, fashioned into intricate designs. The replica earring shown here came from Troy (the original was dated *c.*2300 BC). It was usual for the Greeks to have pierced ears.

REFLECTED BEAUTY

Many people might be surprised at the degree of sophistication enjoyed in Greek society, certainly at the higher levels. Many of the everyday items still currently in use, and which we might regard as modern, had their counterparts in the ancient world, like this bronze mirror. The carving on its stand is the goddess Aphrodite, the goddess of love and beauty. The rear panel was beautifully engraved while the front would have been highly polished to show a reflection. As we do today, most Greeks adorned themselves with make-up and jewellery.

SKIN DEEP

Beauty and personal hygiene were considered very important to the Greeks. Physical exercise and caring for the body was seen as essential to good health. It was fashionable to wash regularly, not in large communal baths, like the Romans, but in small tubs in the privacy of their own houses. They anointed their bodies with olive oil to ensure a good complexion. Both men and women wore perfumes and used cosmetics to colour the skin as a sun tan was considered unattractive. Most people wore hats (like bonnets) as protection from the sun and wore simple, leather sandals on their feet, as worn by this girl on a typical vase decoration.

Art & Architecture

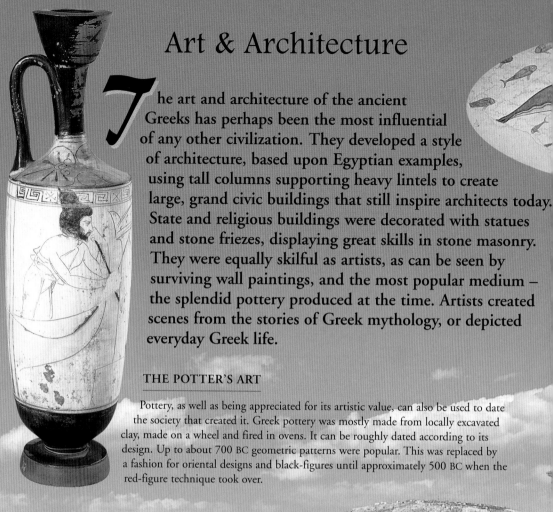

*T*he art and architecture of the ancient Greeks has perhaps been the most influential of any other civilization. They developed a style of architecture, based upon Egyptian examples, using tall columns supporting heavy lintels to create large, grand civic buildings that still inspire architects today. State and religious buildings were decorated with statues and stone friezes, displaying great skills in stone masonry. They were equally skilful as artists, as can be seen by surviving wall paintings, and the most popular medium – the splendid pottery produced at the time. Artists created scenes from the stories of Greek mythology, or depicted everyday Greek life.

THE POTTER'S ART

Pottery, as well as being appreciated for its artistic value, can also be used to date the society that created it. Greek pottery was mostly made from locally excavated clay, made on a wheel and fired in ovens. It can be roughly dated according to its design. Up to about 700 BC geometric patterns were popular. This was replaced by a fashion for oriental designs and black-figures until approximately 500 BC when the red-figure technique took over.

WALL PAINTINGS

The walls of many Greek buildings were adorned with fine frescoes and paintings. The wall painting shown here, depicting dolphins and fish, is a restoration and comes from the Queen's Room in the Palace of Knossos, Crete (*c*.1500 BC).

ARCHITECTURAL STYLES

The dominant features of Greek buildings were the rows of columns supporting the roof beams (lintels). The tops of the columns (capitals) were highly decorated. The three main styles were plain (known as Doric), scroll-topped (Ionic, as shown) or highly decorated with leaf and other designs (Corinthian).

THE ACROPOLIS

The acropolis was the upper fortified section of all Greek cities. This main picture shows the Acropolis in Athens, dominated by the temple of the Parthenon (which means 'virgin'), built between 447 and 432 BC.

Health & Medicine

The Greeks inherited their interest in the study of medicine from the Egyptians, whom they greatly admired. Unlike the Egyptians however, whose physicians specialized in specific areas of the body and treated them in isolation, Greek doctors tended to regard the function of each part in relation to the whole body to promote general good health. They also believed in adopting a good bedside manner and administering a daily dose of wine. Operations to remove infected parts were carried out, but usually only as a last resort. Like so much else in Greek life, health and medicine were dominated by religion. Prayers and offerings were made to the gods, particularly Asclepios. If a patient was cured, they would often leave a model or other token depicting the affected part of the body, as an offering to the gods. It is not known what the average life expectancy was, but certainly the wealthier citizens lived to ages in excess of 70.

THE GOD OF MEDICINE

Asclepios, a son of Apollo, was the god of medicine and healing. Ancient Greeks believed that illness and disease were sent by the gods as a punishment if they were offended. Temples dedicated to Asclepios were amongst the most common in the Greek world, with a special caste of priests practising medicine in his name. In many pagan religions, the serpent (as seen here entwined round his staff) is seen as the 'life-force' flowing through all things and is held sacred.

HEALTHY LIFESTYLES

Sick people travelled many miles to seek cures at the shrines of Asclepios, where the priests prescribed various herbal cures and special diets. One of the principle forms of preventative medicine was exercise, to both appease the gods and generate healthy well-being. Boys were encouraged to practise athletics as training for the army and girls to promote healthy child-bearing.

FOUNDER OF MODERN MEDICINE

Hippocrates (460-377 BC) was a distinguished physician, who was born and studied medicine on the island of Kos. He started teaching in the open, under a plane tree (shown left) – one still grows on the island in commemoration of him. Hippocrates wrote 53 medical books, known as the Corpus. He believed that the human body was a single organism and the individual parts should not be treated separately. He established a code of medical ethics, which doctors still subscribe to today (the Hippocratic Oath).

PERSONAL HYGIENE

The Greeks recognized the importance of personal cleanliness and hygiene to maintain good health. They did not partake in hot and cold plunge baths like the Romans, but did wash frequently in private tubs in their homes. They also used olive oil to deep-cleanse the skin.

SANITATION

From a very early date the Greeks constructed sophisticated water supply and drainage systems. The two systems were kept separate to prevent the spread of disease. Fine examples are to be seen in the palaces and towns of Crete (c.2000 BC) such as Malia and Knossos. Clay pipes buried in the walls distributed clean water from vast reservoirs, while underground channels cut into the stone carried away the waste water.

Love & Marriage

Most marriages in ancient Greece were arranged between both sets of parents. Usually a father would select a husband (often much older) for his daughter when she reached the age of 12 or 13. When courting, a young man would pay a great deal of attention to his intended bride, but once married it was a different story. Wives were considered the property of their husbands and were expected to obey him. Married women were jealously guarded by their husbands and were seldom allowed to meet or talk to other men unless he was present. In Sparta, men were not allowed to marry until the age of 20. The groom had to pretend to carry his bride off, cave-man fashion. To test his courage and initiative the newly-wed Spartan was kept apart from his wife for some time and only allowed to visit her by stealth. If caught, he was punished.

GODDESS OF LOVE

Aphrodite was the Greek goddess of love and beauty. She is nearly always shown as a beautiful young woman, either naked or semi-clothed. On the day of their wedding, brides made offerings to her shrine to ensure a happy marriage.

SPARTAN GIRLS

These young girls come from Sparta, a powerful Greek state that at one time rivalled the power of Athens. In Sparta, the emphasis was on the collective well-being of the state. Both young men and women were encouraged to compete in athletics in order to produce a 'super-race' of soldiers, and so the girls would bear healthy babies. As a result of being treated more as equals, Spartan girls seemed more promiscuous, by comparison, than girls from other states.

VIRTUOUS WIVES

The main purpose in marriage for both a man and a woman was to give birth to sons to carry on the family line. Conversely to the norm, in much of Greece the more wealthy and important a man was, the more restricted his wife was likely to be. She would have been confined to an area of the house called the Women's Quarter. This enabled the man to entertain without the fear of the other guests meeting his wife – whose virtue was paramount. Domestic duties were given to the servants, so rich wives rarely ventured out of the house.

UNREQUITED LOVE

The theme of unrequited love is a common one in Greek mythology, amongst both mortals and the gods. The illustration shown here depicts the sun god, Apollo, and Daphne, a nymph and daughter of the river god, Perseus. Apollo pursued Daphne, but she resisted his advances and asked for help from the king of the gods, Zeus, by praying to him. In answer to her prayers, Zeus turned her into a laurel tree, which afterwards became sacred to Apollo and he often wore a laurel wreath on this head in memory of his lost love. Greek brides often wear laurel wreaths in their hair during the marriage ceremony.

NYMPHS

Nymphs were not gods, but semi-divine female spirits, often associated with nature and fertility. The word 'nymphomania' (excessive sexual desire in women) is derived from the word nymph. In general, the Greeks had a fairly liberal attitude towards sex and nudity, as can be seen in the immodest poses in much of their art and statuary. Women on the island of Lesbos seem to have enjoyed greater freedom than women in other states. They were, for example, allowed a say in choosing their partners and to express themselves in art. Homosexual love was not uncommon in ancient Greece; the word lesbian is derived from Lesbos.

Women & Children

Women in Greek society were very much regarded as second-class citizens and enjoyed few rights. Attitudes varied between the various city-states, but by and large women were held in low regard. Few women were allowed to hold positions of authority and if a woman had money or property these automatically passed to her husband on marriage. Poorer women, unusually, enjoyed more freedom than their rich counterparts, for they at least were allowed to work or meet with friends in the market place. Only sons were treated with any degree of reverence; girls were married off as soon as possible and received no education. There were no schools, as such. The wealthy would pay for private tutors for their sons.

PUT AWAY YOUR CHILDISH THINGS

On reaching the age of 12 children were considered young adults. Boys dedicated their toys to Apollo, girls to his twin sister, Artemis, as a sign of their maturity. Artemis was goddess of the hunt and her shrines were often attended by women.

HELEN OF TROY

Women in ancient Greece were regarded as male possessions, so when Helen (supposedly the most beautiful woman in Greece, and wife of the Spartan king Menelaus) was taken by Paris to Troy, it was considered such a slight that it was one of the rare times that the Greeks became a united army. According to mythology, the Greeks besieged Troy for 10 years to rescue her and the story became the basis for Homer's epic poem, *The Iliad*.

HELD IN THE BALANCE

Greek fathers had the right to decide whether a new-born baby lived or died. If the child was sickly, or if it was a girl, they had the right to abandon the baby if they could not afford to keep it. Such babies were left in the open air to die, though some might be saved by childless families and adopted. Others were rescued, only to become slaves. Those children who survived this harsh judgement were usually well cared for.

CHILDREN AT PLAY

A typical Greek childhood was comparatively short. By the age of 12, boys were often undergoing physical training for the army and girls might already be married. Those children who remained at home after then were expected to help support the family. Children played with a variety of toys, including dolls, soldiers and board games. Greek families were quite large, but child mortality was also quite high. Only about half of those born could expect to reach age 20.

KOUROS

This marble statue of a naked young boy is called a 'kouros'. They were placed in shrines dedicated to Apollo, god of light and healing. There is some evidence to suggest that children were used in certain religious rituals, their innocence symbolizing virtue.

LEARNING BY ROTE

At age 7, boys from rich families began their education. The usual subjects were reading, writing, arithmetic, poetry and music, learnt by reciting out loud. On rare occasions, the daughters of rich families received private tuition. Some tutors would travel between towns and would conduct lessons in the open air. Children from poor families received no education at all.

A WOMAN'S LOT

A woman's lot in ancient Greece was certainly not a happy one. In addition to helping on the family farm, poorer women had to perform many menial tasks, such as cooking, cleaning, spinning and weaving. If a woman did not marry she remained under the control of her father or brothers.

ALEXANDER THE GREAT (356-323 BC)

Alexander became king of Macedon at the age of 20. He went on to become one of the world's greatest leaders. He achieved what no other Greek leader had accomplished, in uniting all the individual city-states into one nation. He built an empire that stretched from Italy in the west, Kashmir in the east and Egypt in the south. He died in Babylon aged just 32. Without his firm leadership, the alliances that he forged between the various city-states weakened and in a short while Alexander's empire collapsed.

STRONGHOLDS

At the centre, and usually the highest point, of every Greek town was a fortified citadel, known as an acropolis. Strong walls and gates protected the main temples and other important buildings from attack in the event of an invasion.

NAVAL POWER

The Greeks relied heavily on the strength of their fleet in retaining mastery of the Aegean Sea, particularly important as many Greek colonies were situated on islands. The fastest and most powerful Greek ship was the *trireme*, which was powered by three tiers of oarsmen, one above the other, on either side. A metal-pointed battering ram was attached to the bows to ram and sink enemy ships.

CHARIOTS

Chariots first appeared in Sumeria and Egypt around 3000 BC. They were small two-wheeled carts pulled by horses and carried two men, a driver and an armed soldier. The Greek army made great use of them, charging the enemy lines and throwing them into disarray.

THE TROJAN WAR

Sieges could last many years, as in the case of Troy (*c.* 1184 BC) which lasted 10 years. The usual practice was to burn the crops surrounding a city and cut off all other supply routes to deny food to the defenders. The combined Greek army eventually won by trickery. Soldiers concealed inside a huge wooden horse, supposedly left behind as a gift to the Trojans, opened the city gates at night letting in the Greek army.

War & Weaponry

Unlike other great civilizations, ancient Greece was never a unified country. For complex reasons of geography and culture, the region developed as a series of independent city-states. Although each of these mini-states was influenced by the others, they were often fiercely independent. Quarrels and wars between the individual states were commonplace and each seems to have taken it in turn to become the most dominant and powerful state. When a war was waged, it was the duty of every male citizen to help fight if needed, as there were no permanent armies, except in Sparta. After the crisis, they returned to their usual work. On only three occasions did the various Greek states unite to act collectively: notably, the Trojan wars of the late 12th century BC; the Persian wars of the 6th and 5th centuries BC; and lastly by Alexander the Great, in the 4th century BC. On the first two occasions they did so out of fear of being conquered. On the last occasion, Alexander united the states by force in order to fulfil his plans of building a Greek empire.

GREEK FIRE

This vase decoration shows Odysseus, a legendary Greek hero, returning from war. Greek ships (called galleys) were quite large and often carried siege engines, such as catapults and ballistas, which could throw projectiles weighing up to 25 kilos. Sometimes, burning missiles made from naphtha, sulphur and saltpetre (known as 'Greek Fire') were hurled amongst enemy ships.

MILITARY SERVICE

There was no standing army in Greece (except in Sparta), but men were trained from age 20 and could be called upon to do military service at any time. Foot soldiers, known as Hoplites, paid for their own equipment which usually consisted of a short sword and spear, with a bronze shield, breastplate and helmet for protection.

Crime & Punishment

Because ancient Greece was not a unified country with one central system of government, it is difficult for us today to understand the complex systems of government and law that operated within the various city-states. Some states, like Lesbos, adopted a much more liberal attitude than more military states, such as Sparta, and this was reflected in their laws. In Athens the ruling classes were driven out and replaced with a democratic system of government and law making. Although only certain classes of citizens had the right to vote, ordinary people were able to make decisions about government for themselves at meetings called 'assemblies'. Not all Greek states adopted the democratic system, however, and many people stood out against it, including the philosopher, Plato. Greece eventually reverted to a monarchical system of government. In the 6th century BC, Solon, a member of the Athens Council, introduced a law giving ordinary citizens the right of appeal against judiciary decisions. By all accounts though, the crime rate generally in Greece was low.

BANKRUPTCY

If a farmer fell upon hard times and got into debt (which happened frequently in ancient Greece when crops often failed in the poor soils) his possessions could be seized and he could be sold into slavery as a bankrupt.

The Athenian politician Solon (c.640-558 BC) shown above, introduced new laws abolishing this practice.

SACRED TEMPLES

To most Greeks, religion was intrinsically entwined with everyday life. The defiling of temples such as this magnificent temple of Apollo in Delphi would have been considered a crime against the entire community. The ultimate fulfilment in life was to serve one's own community and so the ultimate deterrent and punishment for many crimes was banishment, to deny the criminal all the benefits of the Greek way of life. Some crimes, however, such as murder and corruption, were punishable by execution.

DEATH BY POISONING

The teachings of the philosopher Socrates (470-399 BC) were considered so outrageous, even for liberal-minded Greeks, that both government and temple officials considered him a corrupting influence on the young. One principle advanced by him, and copied by Nazi Germany in this century, was selective breeding to produce a super race. He was eventually arrested for his controversial views and was sentenced to death by drinking hemlock.

OSTRACISM

Citizens in the city-state of Athens reserved the right to punish any politician who they thought had behaved badly by banishing them for 10 years. Citizens would cast a vote of no-confidence by writing the person's name on a piece of pottery (as shown here) called an *ostrakon*. The pieces were then counted and if they numbered more than 6,000 the named person was banished. This process was called 'ostracising' and is a term still used today.

PERIKLES

Although Athens adopted the democratic system of government, it did not meet with universal approval. The system was still dominated by powerful statesmen, who could force through laws of their own choosing. The illustration shows Perikles, who was elected 'strategos' (leader of the military) for 14 years in succession, between 443-429 BC.

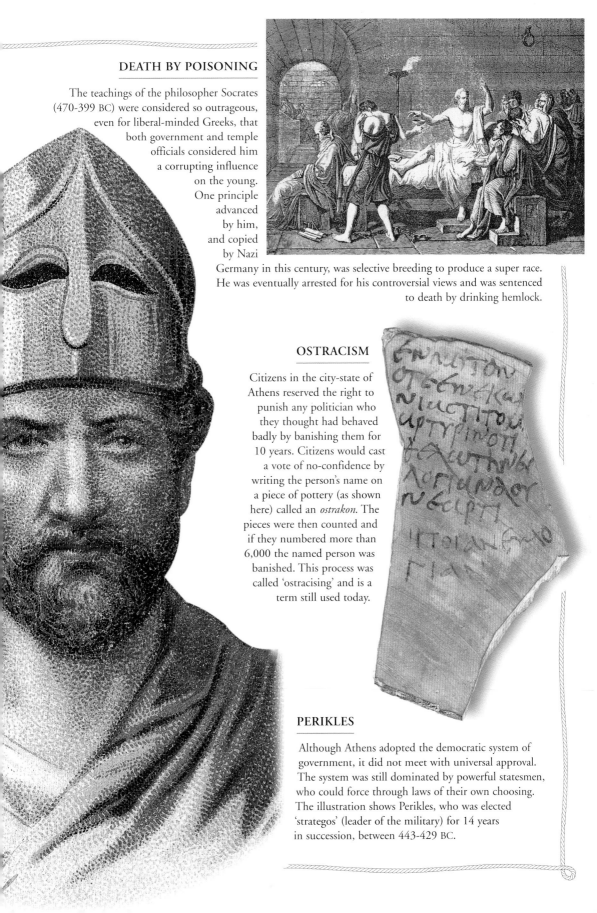

Transport & Science

The Greeks were greatly influenced by the Egyptians, particularly in scientific studies. The sciences then embraced such subjects as religion, the arts philosophy, mathematics, astronomy and astrology, and it is in these areas that the Greeks still affect modern thought today. Perhaps the strongest area of influence, after the arts, has been in philosophical debate. The Greek philosophers were visionary, as were the mathematicians who developed theories concerning atomic principles, before they knew that atoms actually existed. Astronomers also introduced revolutionary theories. As long ago as the 6th century BC, Anaxagoras discovered that the moon did not emanate light, but merely reflected that of the sun. Whilst 300 years later Aristarchus recognized that the sun, not the Earth, was the centre of our solar system.

ROAD TO NOWHERE

Most Greek towns were well serviced with paved roads. These were built with drainage channels and pavements for pedestrians. Some of the earliest examples of roads are to be found in Crete. The example shown here is the Lechaian Road in Corinth. On mainland Greece there were a few long-distance roads, but hardly any linking up the various towns. The mountains made such an enterprise very difficult. For long journeys most Greeks used boats to move around the coast and avoid the hazards of mountain tracks.

MARITIME POWER

Because of its lack of natural resources, Greece relied heavily on trade. Most of the major cities were located on islands scattered across the Aegean and control of the trade routes by sea was essential to maintain the empire.

PLATO

One of the foremost Greek philosophers was Plato (*c.*427-347 BC), who wrote several books discussing the origins of the universe and the relationship between man and the natural world. He lived in Athens and set up a school for philosophers. In addition to teaching (much of which was done by open discussion rather than by lecturing) he also wrote down many of the teachings of Socrates, a fellow philosopher who never actually committed his ideas to paper, preferring the medium of debate.

SEAWORTHY

Sometime around 1600 BC the Minoan civilization, centred on the island of Crete, dramatically improved ship design, making long sea voyages possible. The ships were propelled by the combined use of oars and sails, the manpower usually provided by slaves. Higher prows enabled the ships to cut through the water more easily and a large oar was placed at the stern to act as a rudder.

PYTHAGORAS

To the ancient Greeks, science and religion were inextricably linked, so too were an understanding of art and philosophy. Pythagoras (*c.*580-500 BC) was born on the island of Samos and devoted his life to the study of mathematics. Amongst his theories was the idea that all things in the cosmos were determined by numbers and mathematical relationships. He developed many mathematical principles, especially in geometry, which are still in use today.

TIME-HONOURED TRADITION

This modern photograph shows a peasant woman on the island of Crete leading a donkey along a pack trail. Scenes such as this have hardly changed for centuries. Beasts of burden, such as the donkey, were essential for transport in ancient Greece, where mountain communities were cut off from one another and only accessible along narrow tracks.

PAN

Pan was one of the minor gods.
The son of Hermes, he was
half-man, half-goat, and the
god of shepherds and
flocks. He invented the
pan-pipes and loved
to spend time in the
forest, hunting and
dancing. A mischievous
god, he apparently liked
to startle unwary travellers
and 'panic' them.

KING OF THE GODS

Cronos, youngest son of Uranos (Heaven),
is said to have revolted against his father and
married his sister, Rhea. To prevent his own
sons deposing him he ate each of
his children at birth. When Zeus
was born, Rhea wanted to save
her son and gave Cronos a stone to
swallow instead. When he came of age
Zeus moved to Mount Olympus,
near Macedonia. The twelve main
Greek gods all resided on Olympia.
Zeus became the king of the gods,
and his symbol was thunder.

GODDESS ATHENA

Athena was the daughter
of Zeus and Metis. She was
the goddess of wisdom and
warfare. She was often accompanied by an owl
and presided over the arts, literature, learning and
philosophy. She became the patron goddess of
Athens, the most powerful Greek city-state (which was
so named in honour of her). The temple of the Parthenon in
Athens is dedicated to her.

TEMPLES OF THE GODS

Each of the various Greek gods had their own special
attributes and were worshipped in their own temple. By
appeasing the gods, making offerings or animal sacrifices,
believers hoped to win their favour. Greek towns had
many fine temples, each one splendidly decorated.
Worshippers usually made individual offerings rather
than attend organized services.

Religion

Greek religion was polytheistic, that is they believed in many gods, not just one. The Greeks invented a very complex mythology to explain both the creation of the universe and the origins of the various gods. They saw the world before creation as Chaos, from which sprang the Earth (Ge, or Gaia), who gave birth to the Heavens (Uranos) and the sea (Pontus). The gods were human-like beings who resided on Mount Olympus, and frequently intervened in the affairs of man. Greek religion did not have a moral code. People simply had to appease the gods to get what they wanted from life. If offended, the gods might punish people, but it was not necessary to live a 'good' life in order to be a believer or to receive favour from the gods.

THE FALL OF ICARUS

Daedalus was a mythical craftsman, responsible for many advances in architecture and sculpture. After he killed his nephew, Talos, in a jealous rage, he fled Athens for Crete with his son Icarus. They were later imprisoned by King Minos.

They escaped using wings, fastened to their shoulders with wax, but Icarus flew too close to the sun, melting the wax, and he fell into the sea and drowned.

SON OF ZEUS

Heracles, perhaps the greatest of all heroes, was the son of Zeus by a mortal woman, Alcmene. Although Heracles never became a god himself, he frequently called upon them for their help. He is most famous for his Twelve Labours. When he died he was carried by a cloud to Olympus, where he became immortal and lived with the gods.

GODDESS OF LOVE

The relief above shows Aphrodite the goddess of love, desire and fertility. According to legend she was born out of the sea, either from drops of Uranos's blood, falling from the heavens, or from the union of Zeus and Diane. She possessed a magic girdle, which if given to a mortal made the wearer irresistibly beautiful and desirable.

Legacy of the Past

The sporting ideals created by the Greeks at their great games (particularly the Olympics) live on today. They first developed the idea that it is more important to compete and gain honour for one's community than it is to win.

The civilization that was ancient Greece was by no means the first great civilization; Sumeria, India and Egypt had already flourished and gone into decline long before the founding of the first Greek city-state. However, the founding of Minoan Crete was the first early civilization in Europe. Greek culture flourished around the Aegean Sea, on mainland Greece and eastern Turkey, and on the many islands of the eastern Mediterranean. However, because their civilization was made up of individual city-states, it meant they were often fiercely independent. Had the Greeks ever formed a unified empire they may well have established an even greater civilization. It reached its zenith in the 5th century BC, leaving behind a magnificent legacy of art and architecture, scientific and scholarly research, sports, medicine, philosophy, and a system of government, all of which still form the basis of life today.

THE RENAISSANCE

In 17th-century Europe many architects rejected medieval ideals in building design and looked to the grandeur and elegance of classical Greece as their source of inspiration. The period came to be known as the Renaissance, or 're-birth'.

DEMOCRACY

The governments of the Western World today are founded on the basic principles of democracy, from the Greek words 'demos', meaning people, and 'krakos', meaning power. Democracy was first developed in Athens in the 5th century BC, when a monarchical system of government was replaced by one with elected representatives. The system was not universally supported, however, and not everyone was represented; women, for example, were excluded from voting.

THE ROMAN EMPIRE

The Romans greatly respected the Greeks, modelling their own civilization upon theirs. They especially admired the magnificent yet simple elegance of Greek architecture and used it as the basis for their own style, as can be seen from the Colosseum in Rome.

THE ELGIN MARBLES

For centuries the magnificent remains of classical Greece lay unprotected and uncared for and locals used the buildings as convenient stone quarries. During the 18th and, more particularly, the 19th centuries interest in the ancient world was revived and many sites were excavated. A great many statues and artefacts were rescued and placed in museums around the world. Lord Elgin, a British ambassador, brought back several large sculptures from the Parthenon, in Athens. They can still be seen in the British Museum today.

THEATRE-GOING

Theatre-going was probably started by the ancient Greeks and has remained a popular form of entertainment since those times. Modern theatre design is still based on Greek models with a curved auditorium and seats rising in tiers from front to back.

HERITAGE

Perhaps the ancient Greek's finest legacy is the wealth of art and architectural remains which are a source of inspiration to us today. Sadly, many of these remains have been lost, buried beneath modern towns or deliberately destroyed for the sake of their materials, but enough survives for us to form a picture of the earliest (and some would say greatest) civilization in Europe.

DID YOU KNOW?

That the Greeks invented numerology?
To ancient Greek mathematicians the key to the mysteries of the universe lay in numbers. They devised a 'science', which has come to be known as numerology (and which is still practised today by astrologers) in which each letter of the alphabet was ascribed a number. By using a special reductionist system, every word, or person's name, could be reduced to a single number, which had magical significance, similar to the star signs of the zodiac.

That the word 'platonic' is derived from the Greek philosopher Plato?
Plato believed that it was possible for both men and women to forge deep non-sexual friendships, based entirely on spiritual ideas and nurtured by philosophical debate (Plato actually encouraged women students to take part in debates). Such friendships, sometimes the cause of jealousy and resentment between married couples, are still known as 'platonic'.

That the Greeks first devised a method of measuring the position of a star from Earth? Today we still use this simple, yet very accurate method of measuring the distance of stars from Earth. It is called the parallax method and involves measuring the position of a given star from Earth. The exercise is then repeated at a later date, when the Earth itself would have moved in its orbit round the sun. The distance travelled by the Earth forms the baseline of a triangle, with the two readings of the star forming the base-line angles. By a simple geometric calculation, where the two sides meet gives the distance from Earth of the star.

That attending the theatre once formed part of medical cures? The Greek city of Epidaurus once housed a large shrine to Asclepios, god of medicine and healing. Hospital buildings were located nearby and in the huge amphitheatre, one of the best preserved in Greece, sacred dramas were acted out under direction of the priests, which formed part of the medical cure. People came from miles around to attend these magical plays to cure them of their ills.

That the Greeks sank Roman ships using solar power? In about the year 212 BC the Greek mathematician and inventor, Archimedes, devised a means of defence using giant mirrors. The Roman fleet was sent to attack the port of Syracuse, Archimedes' home town. He instructed soldiers to polish their bronze shields to a high shine and to stand on the quayside in a curved formation to create a huge parabolic mirror. Then, by adjusting the angle of reflection of this mirror, he concentrated the sun's rays and set fire to the Roman ships. The Roman fleet was routed.

ACKNOWLEDGEMENTS

We would like to thank Graham Rich and Elizabeth Wiggans for their assistance.and David Hobbs for his map of the world.
Picture research by Image Select. Printed in China. Copyright © 2003 *ticktock* Publishing Ltd.
First published in Great Britain by *ticktock* Publishing Ltd., Unit 2, Orchard Business Centre, Tunbridge Wells, Kent TN2 3XF. All rights reserved.
No part of this publication may be reproduced, stored in a retrieval system, or transmitted in any form or by any means electronic, mechanical, photocopying, recording or otherwise, without prior written permission of the copyright owner.

A CIP catalogue record for this book is available from the British Library. ISBN 1 86007 580 0

The original Greek spellings have been used where applicable, rather than the sometimes more familiar anglicized spellings

Picture Credits: t=top, b=bottom, c=centre, l=left, r=right, IFC=inside front cover, OBC=outside back cover, OFC=outside front cover
AKG (London); 3cb, 4bl, 5br, 6/7cb, 7r, 7tl, 9tr, 8/9c, 10/11c & OFC, 12bl, 13br, 13t, 12/13ct, 17bl, 18bl, 18/19c, 18tl, 19tr & OFC, 22/23c & OBC, 22bl, 22br, 24bl, 25r, 26b, 26tl, 27tl, 28tr, 28bl, OBC. CFCL/Image Select; 2tl, 27br, 30bl, 30tl. Giraudon; 2b, 4tl, 4tr, 5tr, 10tl, 11r, 12/13cb, 14tl, 14/15ct, 16r, 21br, 21tr, 20/21cb, 29br. Image Select; IFC, 4/5c, 10bl & 32ct & OBC, 10c, 10/11cb, 20/21ct, 20l, 21c, 22tr, 23tr & OFC, 28/29cb, 29cb, 30tr, 31br, 31tr. Pix; OFC (main pic), 2/3c, 3c, 6tl, 6bl, 6r, 6/7cb, 7r, 8t, 9br, 14/15 (main pic), 15tr, 17br. Ann Ronan @ Image Select; 8c, 12tl, 16tl, 17tr, 17tl, 19br, 21cl, 22tl, 23br, 24tl, 24/25c & OBC, 25tr, 27c, 27tr, 28tl, 29tr. Spectrum Colour Library; 30/31c, 31bl. Telegraph Colour Library UK; 8bl.

Every effort has been made to trace the copyright holders and we apologize in advance for any unintentional omissions.
We would be pleased to insert the appropriate acknowledgement in any subsequent edition of this publication.

INDEX